The Scarborough Heritage Trail

Part 1: The Old Town

The site of Newborough Bar. The white three storey building on the right was the residence of William 'Strata' Smith between 1835 and 1839.

Rear Cover;
Dumple Street looking up from the Market prior to demolition in the 1930's, now Friargate.

Front Cover;
St Mary's Street. - early 1900's

CONTENTS

INTRODUCTION

The history of the seaside is effectively mirrored in the history and heritage of Scarborough. Many of the buildings that you will see on the Scarborough Heritage Trail represent milestones on this long and eventful journey from obscure fishing village to thriving seaside town. From the mid 17th century onwards, the far-spreading fame of the medicinal Spa waters brought the rich, the well-connected and the fashionable to Scarborough every season. Much earlier than anywhere else, too, sea bathing became an acceptable feature of the 'Scarborough Experience'. These discerning early visitors sought pleasure as well as health. They demanded - and were prepared to pay for - the best of everything, from accommodation, food and drink to theatrical performances, elegant balls and banquets.

By following the Heritage Trail, you will be able to trace some of the development in the social, religious, literary and artistic life of the rapidly growing town, and the buildings associated with each sphere of activity.

The Heritage Trail also provides a glimpse or two of the earlier medieval walled town, when the narrow streets were thronged with cowled monks and friars as well as with the European seafarers and traders attracted to the busy port for the trade outlets it offered. Later, during the 18th and early 19th centuries, shipbuilding vied in importance with holidaymaking as a major source of economic growth. Here too, the Heritage Trail gives you an insight into the great days of sail as well as of the men who built and owned the ocean-going wooden vessels.

Places, events and people described in this booklet represent a necessarily selective choice of historic sites, mostly located in or near what is now called the 'Old Town', where the traditional fishing community first established itself before the Norman Conquest. Fishing remains an important feature of the local economy today.

Another booklet, covering a much wider area, is planned to complement this publication and will deal with 19th and 20th century Scarborough.

Suggestions for further reading are given on page 27.

A street map, obtainable from the Information Centres located at the corner of Westborough and Valley Bridge Parade (opposite the Railway Station) and on Sandside (near the harbour) will be of help in the location of all places mentioned in this booklet.

1 Grand Hotel

With the arrival of the railway in 1845, Scarborough was well placed to attract a wider spectrum of visitors than ever before. They came now to savour the new-found delights of an established seaside resort, rather than to sample the medicinal Spa waters. The wealthier and more sophisticated of these visitors, who demanded a standard of accommodation and cuisine not hitherto available, were rewarded with a hotel that excelled any other throughout Europe at that time, either in situation, size or range of amenities. Its lofty and spacious ground floor lounge still retains some of the aura of a more expansive age.

The locally funded Scarborough Cliff Hotel Company engaged the well-known architect, Cuthbert Brodrick, who designed Leeds Town Hall, Leeds Corn Exchange and the Town Hall at Hull, to design a magnificent building on 12 floors and with 365 rooms, towering 160 feet above the sea. The St. Nicholas Cliff site alone cost the company £30,000.

In 1865, with the hotel less than half completed, the Scarborough Cliff Hotel Company went into liquidation. A Leeds businessman, Archibald Neil, bought both site and building at auction for the knock-down price of £43,000. Work then went ahead once more, still to the original plans of Cuthbert Brodrick. By 1867, the Grand Hotel was ready for occupation and was reputed to be the largest and most advanced hotel in Europe.

With its four distinctive domes (representing the seasons of the year), it still dominates the South Bay seafront. It has survived bombardment by the German fleet in December 1914, several changes of ownership and as many financial crises.

The Grand Hotel moved into more tranquil waters financially in 1978 when it was acquired by Butlins Ltd. and once again enjoyed the high occupancy rates of its Victorian heyday though catering for a very different clientele. The hotel has recently been taken over by the Grand Hotel Group Ltd.

The Grand Hotel, once the finest hotel in all Europe, still dominates Scarborough's South Bay skyline

2 Anne Brontë

Scarborough held a special appeal for Anne Brontë, youngest of the three famous Brontë sisters. She made three or four visits, and it was here that she chose to come from her Haworth home in the final stages of her last fatal illness (tuberculosis). Thanks to a legacy of £200 from her godmother, Anne could afford to stay at her favourite lodgings in the fashionable St. Nicholas Cliff area - on a site where the Grand Hotel now stands - and to pay the expenses of her elder sister, Charlotte, as well as Charlotte's old school friend, Ellen Nussey. (They were charged 30 shillings a week each for their lodgings).

The three of them arrived at No. 2, The Cliff on 25th May 1849, where Anne was able to enjoy for the last time the incomparable views. Within three days, she was dead. Because St. Mary's Parish Church was undergoing restoration at the time, Anne's funeral service was held at nearby Christ Church in Vernon Road (located just above the public library until 1979, when it was demolished).

Anne Brontë's grave in St. Mary's Church yard.

Ellen Nussey registered Anne's death and mistakenly entered her age as 28, instead of 29, an error not since rectified on the tombstone in St. Mary's Churchyard (see page 24). Charlotte complained later about this and other errors in the inscription. The local Civic Society has erected a plaque on the Grand Hotel near the main entrance where No. 2 The Cliff once stood.

As Acton Bell, Anne Brontë wrote two books – 'The Tenant of Wildfell Hall' and 'Agnes Grey'. She also left us 59 poems, which are perhaps her greatest gift to posterity.

No more than 100 yards from the Grand Hotel you will find Scarborough's oldest hotel, the Royal, on St. Nicholas Street, well-known to 18th century visitors as the Long Room.

3 The Long Room and Royal Hotel

By 1725, the Long Room was established at the seaward end of Long Room (St. Nicholas) Street, replacing two previous long rooms that existed on Sandside and Princess Street. Reputedly designed by the Earl of Burlington, who had earlier planned the Assembly Rooms at York, the 1725 Long Room boasted an 'Egyptian Hall', 112 feet long, 40 feet wide and 40 feet high. This massive room was the elegant setting for the Grand Balls held regularly during the 18th century seasons. You could also dine in some style, and play billiards and card games. In effect, the Long Room was an upper class non-residential social club for Scarborough's well-heeled visitors. In 1733 it cost five shillings a year to join and one shilling for an evening attendance. The original 18th century Long Room probably occupied the site of the present day Royal Hotel ballroom.

The Long Room was purchased by a Mr. Edward Donner towards the turn of the century, and became popularly known as 'Donner's Rooms' to early 19th century visitors. It seems that Donner added bedrooms to the building in the 1820's still incorporating the original Long Room. He sold out around 1840 and the Royal Hotel begins to be mentioned from this time onwards. Edward Donner's former house in St. Nicholas Street was absorbed into the hotel in

1847, and a new block by the architect Henry Wyatt was added on the Harcourt Place frontage in 1862. The present day dining room was constructed in 1935 on a site formerly occupied by the billiards room.

The Royal's entrance hall and main staircase, in the oldest part of the building, provide a reminder of the elegance of a bygone age. For 30 years, the hotel was owned and managed by the Laughton family (from 1935 onwards). The late Mr. Tom Laughton purchased and hung many paintings by major artists in the public rooms. (Some of these paintings are included in the Tom Laughton Collection at the Crescent Art Gallery, at the far end of The Crescent itself).

In 1975 Mr. Robert Luff, a London theatrical impresario, acquired the hotel and spent £1 million on refurbishing the building. More recently, the Royal has been taken over by English Rose Hotels.

The Royal Hotel stands on the site of the former Long Room, the fashionable hub of Scarborough's social life during the 18th century seasons.

The Royal Hotel is a Grade II listed building.
In 2003 there were 1960 listed items
in the Borough of Scarborough,
including 26 Grade I and 86 grade II* buildings.

Queen Victoria's Statue in the Town Hall Gardens. Once the private home of a prominent local banker, the Jacobean-style Town Hall was purchased by Scarborough Corporation in 1898.

4 The Town Hall (formerly St. Nicholas House)

The Town Hall, just across the street from the Royal Hotel, was built in the mid 19th century as a residence for John Woodall, a member of a prominent family of Scarborough bankers. The bank itself – Woodall, Hebden & Co. – moved to the corner of Newborough and St. Nicholas Street in 1864. The building was designed by Henry Wyatt. Barclays Bank took over the business in 1896 and still occupy the site. The style of the Town Hall is Jacobean, designed in 1852 by Henry Wyatt (who also designed the Gothic pavilion at the Spa). The original owner's initials may be seen in the gable end high above the main entrance. The house was probably completed in 1846-1847; this seems to be confirmed by a rather ornate 1844 in the initialled plaque.

John Woodall died on 9th February 1879 and was succeeded by his son John W. Woodall, who offered the house and associated gardens to the Corporation in 1898. The decision as to where to site the new Town Hall was resolved at a meeting on 5th April 1898, when the Corporation decided to buy St. Nicholas House. Harry W. Smith, the recently appointed borough engineer and surveyor, designed a new eastern (seaward) wing in a broadly similar style to the original, to accommodate the council chamber and other offices. This work was completed in 1903. He also redesigned the Cliff gardens, opened to the public on 14th August 1900. Subsequently, on the 12th December 2001, the St. Nicholas Cliff gardens were reopened again after substantial regeneration. Harry Smith went on to lay out or redesign most of Scarborough's parks and pleasure grounds during the next 30 years, including Peasholm Park and the Italian Gardens on the South Cliff. Further alterations to the Town Hall were made in 1962-64, with extensions in King Street and St. Nicholas Street.

The statue of Queen Victoria in the Town Hall gardens is the only statue of a public figure to be found in Scarborough.

5 Theakston's Bookshop

Walking a few yards further along St. Nicholas Street brings you to Solomon Theakston's former bookshop at No. 31, now an entrance to Marks and Spencer's store. Theakston was a 19th century Scarborough 'institution', well patronised by both residents and visitors during his period of ownership from 1841 to 1875. He was neither the first nor the only bookseller in town, but certainly ended up as the best known. Theakston, a native of York, opened a library and bookshop across the street at No. 6 in 1828. He transferred the expanding business to larger premises on the other side at No. 31 in 1841.

The move enabled him to house not only his wife and himself, but also an amazing variety of enterprises behind the Georgian façade of the building, which had originally been a lodging house. From 1845 onwards, he printed and published on the premises the weekly 'Scarborough Gazette', with its accompanying list of visitors, as well as a popular guide book to the town which ran into many editions between 1840 and 1881. In addition to the library and bookshop, he set up a fine arts gallery, where H. B. Carter, a celebrated painter of local scenes and seascapes, exhibited and sold many of his works. Tickets for the Spa Theatre were on sale at Theakston's; you could also buy wallpaper there, and even arrange to collect your mail at No. 31.

When Solomon Theakston died childless in 1875, aged 64, his former clerk, John Haygard, continued all the business activities until 1895. The Theakston 'empire' then went gradually into decline and was ultimately acquired by W. H. Smith and Son Limited. From 1904 W. H. Smith's traded as booksellers and stationers at the premises until moving to a new purpose-built shop on Westborough in 1981.

The site was then purchased by Marks and Spencer and incorporated in a major store extension. The present St. Nicholas Street frontage is a faithful replica of the late 18th century building, just as Theakston would have known it 160 years ago. Marks and Spencer gained a local Civic Society award for this work.

When you reach the end of St Nicholas Street, turn left on to the Newborough pedestrian precinct and walk as far as North Street. This marks the historic site of the original Newborough Bar.

6 Newborough Bar

From medieval times, Scarborough was a walled and moated town. Newborough Bar was the centrepiece of these fortifications and the principal point of entry. It was probably erected before the reign of Henry III and was rebuilt in 1642. Newborough Bar also served as a local prison for several centuries, refractory and drunken prisoners being confined on the north side of the bar, debtors on the south side next to the gaoler's lodgings.

It was last fortified in 1745, when 6 guns were mounted on either side of Newborough Bar. The guns were never fired in action, and the bar reverted to its penal function for the next 100 years. When the prisoners were transferred to more secure and less insanitary premises, first in Castle Road and then to the 'model' prison in Dean Road designed by the architect W. B. Stewart and built in1866 (still surviving in a different role as a Council stores depot), Newborough Bar had outlived its useful purpose.

It was demolished in 1847 and replaced by the purely ornamental Newborough Bar, designed by John Barry. This imposing neo-Gothic castellated structure, impeded the growing traffic flow along the town's main street. It was bought by the Corporation in 1890 and knocked down.

At the end of North Street the building that stands next to the site of Newborough Bar was formerly the Bar Hotel (subsequently to be known as the Huntsman Pub). On the wall of this building can be found a plaque along with a fixture for the Pancake Bell (dated 1996). The bell, which is placed in situ on Shrove Tuesday, is rung to start the annual pancake race. This bell is a comparative new edition of the original 'curfew' bell, which is on display at the Rotunda Museum at the seaward end of Valley Road.

Now retrace your steps down the Newborough pedestrian precinct and turn left on to St Thomas Street. Just before Chapman, Preston & Hastie's (CPH) estate agency on the right stood a famous theatre for nearly 200 years.

7 Theatre Royal

Scarborough can claim one of the longest theatrical traditions of any town in the country outside London. When the old Theatre Royal on Tanner (now St. Thomas) Street closed in 1924, it marked the end of approaching 200 years of theatrical performances on that site. A guide book of 1734 refers to the theatre (then no more than a tented booth) as an already established feature, with a Mr. Kerregan bringing a theatrical company from York 'every season'. After taking the Spa waters in the morning, the nobility and gentry liked to while away the afternoon at the theatre. Later, they took a leisurely stroll back down Long Room (St. Nicholas) Street to dine, dance and gamble the night away at the Assembly Rooms (see page 5).

One of the several owner-managers was Stephen George Kemble, brother of the celebrated Mrs.

Siddons, who performed at the Theatre Royal, with all the other theatrical 'greats' of the 19th century. Visitors could expect to see famous names like Charles Kemble, Edmund Kean, William Charles MacReady and Ellen Terry topping the bill. Earlier, in 1781, the playwright Sheridan had written a comedy entitled 'A Trip to Scarborough'.

As the number of visitors increased during the 19th century, the compact 18th century theatre became too small to cope. Henry Mayhew, the enterprising owner-manager between 1886 and 1919, enlarged the building considerably in the 1880's to accommodate audiences of over 1,000. The theatre survived somewhat precariously until 1924.

Later, the building was purchased by

Scarborough Corporation and was demolished under a road-widening scheme.

Nothing remains today to remind the passer-by of this 200 year old Thespian tradition, and only a dwindling band of older Scarborians can now recall the final years of the old Theatre Royal.

Retrace your steps to Newborough, and turn left down this hilly road leading to the Old Town area. The second road on your right is Bland's Cliff. Walk a few yards down this steep and narrow cobbled street until you reach the Bell Hotel, set back on the right of Bland's Cliff.

8 The Bell Hotel

There has been an inn, known first as the Blue Bell Inn, near the top of the serpentine Bland's Cliff since at least 1776. Later, as the Bell Hotel, it was one of Scarborough's principal coaching inns.

The Bell not only accommodated those who came to sample the Spa waters but was also the station for the prestigious daily Royal Mail coach to York, among other regular coaching services. When the railways overtook the horse-drawn coaches, the nobility and gentry had already moved elsewhere to seek their pleasures, and the Bell was forced to adjust to changing circumstances. In 1839, the 'commercial gentlemen' who serviced the expanding town's many trade outlets, could obtain full board – with 'mountains' of food included – for six shillings a day.

One such distinguished guest was Dr Granville, the celebrated 'Spa traveller'.

As the 19th century progressed, holidaymakers also helped to fill the hotel's bedrooms right up to the late 1930's.

A reminder of the bustling coaching days can still be found in the adjacent Prospect Place. Note the clipped brickwork on the end wall of No. 7, where careless coachmen sometimes misjudged the distance. Together, the four-square Bell Hotel and Prospect Place make up a unique 18th century enclave on the edge of the Old Town area.

Another former coaching inn (now flats and offices) was the Talbot Hotel in Queen Street. You will pass it on the way back to town at the end of the Heritage Walk.

Returning now to Newborough, cross the street and enter St. Helen's Square, which is almost opposite Bland's Cliff. You can now see the massive proportions of the 19th century Market Hall on the right-hand side.

Bell Hotel 2004 awaiting a new use.

Although built in 1853, the Market Hall is still a pleasing feature of St. Helen's Square and remains a busy shopping centre.

9 Market Hall

Before the construction of the Market Hall in 1853, weekly markets were held in various parts of Scarborough, each often associated with one commodity. For example, Newborough was the Thursday Market, at which pots, glass and earthenware goods were on sale from Bar Street down to St. Nicholas Street; and stalls of general goods on both sides of the street further down to St. Helen's Square. On Saturdays, a market was held in Princess Street.

The new Market Hall was built by a private market company and opened on 8th August 1853. Annual Street fairs were still held, however, at Martinmas and Whitsuntide; with the tolls now passing to the market company. An Order of the Home Secretary in November 1896 terminated all the surviving annual fairs held in Newborough. The market company was paid £300 compensation by the Corporation for loss of all these tolls. A copy of the 1896 Order can

11

be seen in the Rotunda Museum. One street market – that of the corn merchants - persisted in nearby King Street until the 1950's, however.

The market building was designed by John Irvin, Borough Surveyor (who died less than three months before it opened) and cost £16,000. Despite its down-to-earth purpose, it is a dignified building with pleasing lines, mercifully unmodified since erection. The two decorative borough seals on the front elevation possess a special charm.

Scarborough Fair, now celebrated in the song popularised by Simon and Garfunkel, flourished for over 500 years. Between 15th August and 29th September every year, the annual herring fish fair was held mainly on the sands. It also extended to the narrow streets and alehouses of the Old Town which were crowded with local tradesmen and European merchants, as well as minstrels, fortune tellers, quack doctors and dentists, and many others. Scarborough Fair had faded into history by the end of the 18th century and was last held in 1778, though still very much alive in local folklore.

Walk now to the rear of the Market Hall - either along the adjacent Market Way or through the Market Hall itself - and you are at the top of St. Sepulchre Street. About 200 yards down this street on your right is Trinity House. It can be identified by the superior stone facing and the lettering across the width of the façade at second-storey level.

10 Trinity House

One of the few properties in Scarborough designated as a Grade II* listed building (the star denotes a particularly important building), Trinity House has played a significant role in the seafaring life of the town. It is one of only four such establishments in the country, the others are at London, Hull and Newcastle-upon-Tyne, and its foundation reflects the importance of Scarborough as a port in the early 17th century. The original Society of Ship Owners and Master Mariners (35 of the former and 39 ships' captains) built almshouses on the St. Sepulchre Street site, and later bought the land itself for £100 in 1665. A gift, left by Admiral Sir John Lawson (circa 1616 to 1665) in his will to the poor of Scarborough, funded the erection of the first Trinity House. It contained 27 apartments for aged or maimed seamen and/or their widows, as well as 'two fine rooms' in which the trustees could hold their meetings. These trustees had to be either ship-owners, master mariners or naval officers, a requirement, which still applies today.

An Act of Parliament of 1747 created a merchant seamen's fund to finance such charitable institutions, financed by a levy of 6d (2$\frac{1}{2}$ pence) a month from all persons employed on any vessel belonging to the four ports involved. During the five-year period from 1747 to 1752, over £1,000 was raised locally by the levy – an enormous sum in those days. This fund financed the construction of the Merchant Seaman's Hospital opened in 1752 on the site of the current fire station. Even Scarborough Corporation found it convenient to borrow money from Trinity House!

First erected in 1602 and re-built in 1832 Trinity House was once the centre of Scarborough's maritime trade

In this building, the entire business of the port was conducted: ships were bought and sold in the impressive first-floor board room that remains a notable feature of the interior, cargoes arranged, insurances effected and indentures signed.

Rebuilt in 1832 to the designs of R. H. Sharp of York, Trinity House is a fine example of classical style architecture in ashlar-faced stone. Behind this distinguished frontage are now seven, self-contained modern flats, housing retired seamen and their dependants. The historic board room is lit by three chandeliers given by the Belfast descendants of Edward Harland (of Harland and Woolf fame) who, as a schoolboy, watched 'splendid East Indiamen of some 1,000 tons burden' being built at Scarborough shipyards of the Tindall family (see page 20). This boardroom, with its numerous maritime mementoes, is still used for the statutory bi-annual meetings of the 15 trustees.

Trinity House also controls an annexe of 18 flats on Tollergate, rebuilt in 1959, although there were seamen's almshouses on the site from 1752. Wilson's Mariners Homes on Castle Road, designed by John Barry, were founded and endowed by Richard Wilson - himself a former trustee of Trinity House - in 1836. They are typical single-storey almshouses built in the Gothic Style.

Now carry on walking down St Sepulchre Street, crossing to the left-hand side, until you come to a small garden area - now sadly neglected - behind tall iron railings. This was a Quaker burial ground in front of the early 19th century meeting house built by the Quakers of the time.

11 The Old Quaker Meeting House

Quakers meetings for worship were held in Scarborough from 1651 onwards and weddings were known from 1661. Quakers would not take part in normal civil or religious wedding ceremonies. Instead, they performed their own marriages in front of witnesses and they took good care to publicise such proceedings, as an insurance against gossip. Early meetings were held in private homes and often resulted in heavy fines being imposed on the householder concerned.

George Fox, a pioneer of the movement, was imprisoned in Scarborough Castle from 1665 to 1666.

A perennial problem was the Quaker's attitude to carrying arms. Several of the Tindall shipbuilding family (see page 20) were Quakers but after the barque 'Morning Star' was scuttled by pirates in 1828, Robert Tindall ordered that henceforward all Tindall ships should be armed; as a consequence, he left the Society of Friends (Quakers).

In 1676, what was probably the second meeting house was opened in Low Conduit Street (now Princess Square). This was replaced by the St. Sepulchre Street building in 1801, which in turn was replaced by new premises in York Place in 1894. This was demolished in 1990 to make way for the Brunswick Pavilion Development. The new Quaker meeting house is located in Woodlands Drive near Scarborough General Hospital. The St. Sepulchre Street building shows the characteristic plain exterior of such places, reflecting the Quakers' simple philosophy of life. Note the simple stones in the burial ground, with the minimum of information.

You are now on the edge of Princess Square. Proceed to its far right-hand corner, and turn into West Sandgate, where you will find the remnants of the historic Butter Cross, protected by a formidable circlet of iron railings.

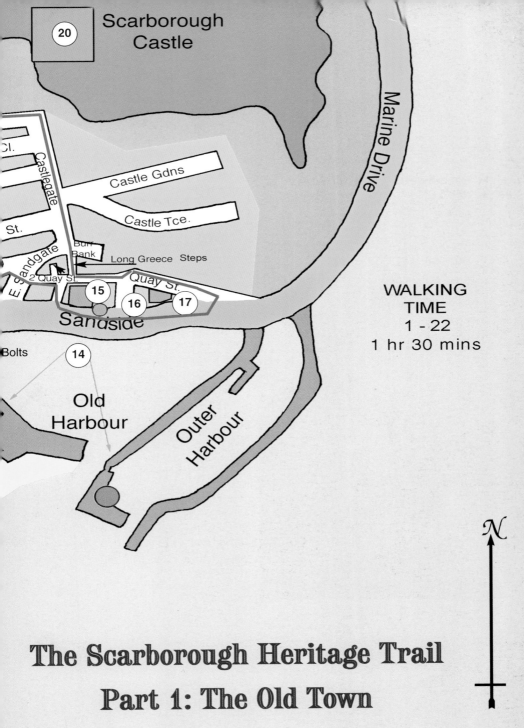

The Scarborough Heritage Trail
Part 1: The Old Town

12 Butter Cross

Almost every street junction in Scarborough during the Middle Ages was the site of a stone cross, erected by the more wealthy burgesses as evidence of their religious piety. Perhaps these crosses were also intended as an atonement for sharp trading practices. Only one survives in the 21st century - the Butter Cross, at the junction of West Sandgate and Princess Square.

The Butter Cross on West Sandgate was probably first erected near the present-day Market Hall. For several centuries it was the focal point of street markets in the town.

Although now only an anachronistic and eroded symbol of a long-vanished past, the Butter Cross was once both a useful and practical object in the town's daily life. Believed to date from Edward VI reign, it has stood on or near this site ever since.

In earlier days, the Butter Cross probably did duty as an anchoring point for sheets, which provided some shelter for open-air traders. Market officials collecting tolls on transactions would have found it equally convenient for sheltering from the weather. Because a Market Cross was an accepted meeting place, visiting preachers would sometimes use it as a base and the town crier (formerly known in Scarborough as a Bell Man) would read official proclamations there. When the Cross lost its headpiece is not recorded.

Opposite the remnants of the once richly carved Butter Cross is perhaps the most visually attractive public house in Scarborough still surviving. The Leeds Hotel was built in 1693 and restored with careful attention to detail in 1900 to a design by Frank A. Tugwell. Note the elaborate woodwork finish to the upper storey and the pleasing inn sign at ground floor level, lettered in Art Nouveau style.

From West Sandgate, where both the Butter Cross and the Leeds Hotel are situated, carry on downhill the few yards to busy Eastborough. You should look now for a narrow alleyway on your left, which is signposted by its ancient name of The Bolts.

13 The Bolts

Surviving relics of medieval town life are as hard to come by in Scarborough as anywhere else. There is one unique feature, however, still existing just behind the seafront razzmatazz of modern Sandside to remind us of that long vanished world. The Bolts are a series of narrow, poorly lit passageways running intermittently behind the seafront cafés and amusement arcades.

In 1225, Henry III made a grant of forty oaks to construct a new quay and houses were erected on the new won land, however, the existence of long established rights of way ensured that the The Bolts did not disappear beneath the new buildings.

Emerging from The Bolts at the beginning of Quay Street, the old house at the junction with Whitehead Hill (No. 2 Quay Street) is another survivor from an earlier age. It probably dates from the late 15th century and is a timber-framed gabled building, the timbers of the second storey jutting out to support the gable. The windows are all of later construction and the half timbering, once concealed with lath and plaster, is now visible again between the modern pebbledash finish. No 2. Quay Street was restored in 1965 and provides a solitary reminder of how this ancient street looked in Elizabethan times, when it was the principal thoroughfare of Scarborough.

The Bolts looking east towards East Sandgate

After this glimpse of Quay Street from Whitehead Hill, turn right and walk the few yards down to the harbour area on the seafront.

In addition to the dark blue 'Heritage Trail' plaques, you may see lighter blue plaques around the town, marking Scarborough's connections with notable people. There are plaques to Sir George Cayley (Paradise) Wilfred Owen (Clifton Hotel), H B Carter (York Place), Charles Laughton (West Square), Sir Edward Harland (Newborough - Marks & Spencer), William 'Strata' Smith (Newborough/Bar Street), Lord Leighton (Brunswick Centre), Sir Edwin Cooper (Nelson Street), Anne Brontë (Grand Hotel) and the Sitwells (Wood End).

14 The Harbour, Piers and Lighthouse

Since earliest recorded time, Scarborough's livelihood depended on the safe haven provided by the curve of sandy beach protected by the vast bulk of the Castle headland. Successive English Kings made grants for harbour works from 1225 onwards, recognising the strategic importance of a strong maritime base. King Richard III, a frequent visitor to Scarborough both before and during his short reign (see page 19) stationed warships in the port. These were the forerunners of the modern fishery protection service, and they took part in the first 'cod war' with Iceland as long ago as 1484.

During the 15th and 16th centuries, the port went into a decline. Only the fishing fleet and the transport of sea-coal kept it alive. Queen Elizabeth I granted £500, one hundred tons of timber and six tons of iron for the strengthening of the outer pier. It was severely damaged in the great storm of 1613 and subsequently repaired and maintained out of sea-coal money granted in

1614. William Vincent was responsible for an extension to the old pier and this was completed in 1752. From this date work began on the 1380 foot long East Pier which cost £12,000 and was not completed until 1826. The massive stones used in its construction, weighing up to 30 tons apiece, were quarried locally and positioned manually. Convicts were among those employed on this massive project. Smeaton's design has withstood North Sea gales since the early 19th century.

The West Pier was begun shortly afterwards, using stone from the then redundant inner island pier. The inner pier was finally demolished in 1880. All the fishing activity of the modern port, including a daily fish market is now concentrated on the West Pier. Here you will see the local cobles and larger keel-boats off-loading their catches and taking on fresh supplies. The North Wharf, adjoining Sandside, was built in 1926, when the herring trade was approaching its

The 'Coronia' pleasure boat entering Scarborough Harbour.

zenith. In those colourful days, Scottish fisher lasses came South in their hundreds to gut, fillet and pack in tubs the rich herring harvest of the North Sea. It is said that you could walk across the inner harbour from end to end across the decks of the tightly packed fishing trawlers.

In 1804, the first recorded lighthouse on Vincent's Pier consisted of a flat roofed building with a brazier on top as the only warning signal. The purpose of the lighthouse at this time was to warn ships of the available depth of water in the harbour. Tallow candles, oil lamps and gas were used successively to provide a better light. The engineer Robert Nixon built a brick lighthouse at the harbour in 1806. By 1850, the lighthouse had acquired a second storey and its familiar domed top. Modern electric lighting gives a visibility of nine miles for the powerful beam. During the 1914 German Bombardment, a shell sliced through the lighthouse tower. It had to be dismantled to first floor level, and was rebuilt by public subscription in 1931.

As ships increased in both size and numbers built during the late 18th century, there were far more shipwrecks around our coasts during stormy weather, many of them happening in sight of a safe harbour. These tragedies led to the development of a lifeboat service. Scarborough's first lifeboat station was on the foreshore, near the present underground car park at the approach road to the Spa. Thomas Hinderwell, Scarborough's first serious historian, helped to secure the town's first lifeboat. The station was moved to the harbour area in 1821, firstly on the landward side of the present Foreshore Road, and latterly on the seaward side. From 1801 to 1984, there have been 567 launches of the Scarborough Lifeboat and 441 lives saved. A total of 16 lifeboatmen were lost during this period. The worst loss of life to the lifeboat crew since the last war was when the lifeboat overturned approaching the harbour on 8th December 1954, and three crewmen were swept overboard and drowned.

Strolling along Sandside in the direction of the Castle and Marine Drive, you will come across an old stone building, known as King Richard III's house, now used as a restaurant.

15 King Richard III House

Richard Plantagenet is reputed to have stayed at this house on Sandside when he was Lord High Admiral to his brother, King Edward IV. When he became king, Richard III radically reorganised our sea defences and is credited with being the founder of the English navy in the modern sense. By this time, he was living in Scarborough Castle on his visits to the town. When the 'Navy of the North' was based at Scarborough Harbour, Richard apparently took command of the fleet at least once, when it was engaged in naval warfare with the Scottish Fleet. He granted a wide-ranging charter to Scarborough during his short reign (1483-85).

King Richard III house is said to incorporate medieval stone walls, indicating a much larger early building. The present structure shows only Elizabethan features, though the late Sir Nikolaus Pevsner said that only the mullioned and transomed windows on the side wall are original; those on the frontage were constructed in 1914 to what is believed to have been the original design. The replacement stonework of that date is easily distinguishable from the earlier weathered fabric of the house's frontage.

Inside King Richard III's house, the principal feature worthy of note is the ornamental plaster ceiling in the upper room known as the King's bedchamber, though installed long after his death. Its centrepiece is the rose of York – Richard's family emblem.

King Richard III House on Sandside.

There was a shipyard in front of King Richard III's house during the 18th and 19th centuries and many others in both directions in the days when shipbuilding was important locally. All traces of the shipyards, the numerous slipways and the associated warehouses and chandlers' stores have vanished.

Continue along Sandside towards the Castle & Marine Drive until you pass the Golden Ball. Plaque is on adjoining brick building.

16 Shipbuilding in Scarborough

John Cockerill and his brother James had slipways on the Scarborough waterfront during the middle and late 17th century. The Cockerills were a well-established shipbuilding family, who intermarried with the Tindall family and eventually the two concerns became amalgamated. Seven generations of Tindalls were involved in shipbuilding, finishing with Richard who died in 1862, after which the yard was closed. Smaller boats were still built in the harbour by other yards until 1885.

The busiest period for the Tindall yards was between 1771-1800, under the direction of John Tindall (1755-1809), when 100 vessels were built. Then, shipyards lined the waterfront from Bland's Cliff to Old Pier. One of the Tindall yards was adjacent to the Old Pier; another was in front of King Richard III's house. Many of the warehouses and workshops associated with

shipbuilding were lost firstly with the completion of Foreshore Road in 1877 and later in the clearing of the old Sandside area in 1902.

Paintings in the Crescent Art Gallery by H. B. Carter, Ernest Dade and Atkinson Grimshaw, among others, convey an excellent impression of the local maritime scene during the 19th century.

When iron and steel replaced wood in ship construction, Scarborough faded quite rapidly from the shipbuilding scene and from shipowning, too.

Continue along Sandside until you reach the roundabout at the beginning of the Marine Drive. Turn sharp left into Quay Street and walk along this quaint and narrow street until you reach the Three Mariners Inn on your left.

17 The Three Mariners Inn

Arguably the earliest licensed premises in Scarborough (though the Newcastle Packet on nearby Sandside is a rival claimant) the Three Mariners is certainly one of the oldest buildings in town. On the west side of the building you can see a gable in the shape of an inverted V as well as a square frame, suggesting a medieval origin, possibly of around 1300. The Quay Street façade is a much later addition in the 17th century, giving the building something of a doll's house appearance. Note the external decoration: above each window and door are pediments (chevrons in brick) to give these features prominence. However, these 'eyebrows' do not sit directly above their respective doors or windows. Instead, a projecting course of brickwork (a string course) has been added, for extra emphasis. The doorway is late 18th century.

Legend has it that the Three Mariners Inn was once the haunt of smugglers. It certainly does have a smuggler's cupboard in the chimney breast and it did have an underground passage to the arches at the back of the quay, passable only at low tide. Furthermore, it is reputed to have no fewer than 26 cupboards in the house, many of them connected with secret hiding places. Once known as 'The Blockmaker's Arms', this name suggests an association with the great shipbuilding era of later years.

During Victorian times, it was a favoured haunt for the many artists who found the nearby harbour area an endless source of inspiration. The figurehead above the side entrance to the building is a replica.

Be prepared next for a fairly stiff climb up the slopes of Castle Hill. Continue along Quay Street until a flight of steps can be seen on open space to the right. Ascend Long Greece Steps and carry on up Castlegate until the road turns to the left. Paradise House is the large grey painted building on your left.

The Three Mariners Inn is probably the earliest licensed house in town, c.1300. Note the medieval timber framework on the end wall.

Paradise House; looking towards the Castle

18 Paradise House

'Paradise' in medieval times meant a monastic walled garden, which is just what the 12th century French Cistercian monks created on the sloping site below and to the east of St. Mary's Church. When Henry IV ended that association in 1405, by giving custody of the parish church to Bridlington Priory, little is known about subsequent development of the Paradise site. By 1690, however, John Cockerill (see page 20), was living there in a substantial gabled house built in the Jacobean style. A century later, Paradise House and its tree-lined garden were notorious as the haunt of smugglers. An observant chronicler, William Hutton, writes in 1803 of ' a deep draw well, covered by a small outhouse' behind Paradise, which had a 'room of considerable magnitude hollowed out of the rock'. It was here that 'a nest of smugglers' outwitted the excisemen by depositing their illicit goods in what was private property. Sir George Cayley, 'the Father of Aeronautics', is widely believed to have been born here in 1773, but Cayley himself later claimed Long Room

(St. Nicholas) Street as his birthplace.

In 1856, Paradise House resumed its shipbuilding connections when young Richard Tindall set up home there. The Tindalls were by now related to the Cockerills by marriage and the two businesses had merged. East Mount, as the property was renamed by Richard Tindall, remained in the family's ownership until the First World War. Struck by a shell in the German Bombardment of 1914, the building and grounds were purchased by Christopher Colborne Graham, Mayor of Scarborough from 1913 to 1919. Mr. Graham gave the property to the Council's Education Committee, who reopened Paradise House as the Graham Sea Training School in 1917. Thus it remained for the next 55 years, training several generations of local fishermen and merchant seamen in the art and science of seamanship. The building has now been converted to flats.

Ahead of you at the end of Paradise, the parish church of St. Mary's is now clearly visible.

19 St. Mary's Parish Church

No building in Scarborough has a longer or more turbulent history than the 800-year old parish church of St. Mary's near the top of Castle Road. A church has probably occupied this commanding position even before the first castle was erected. The first single aisled structure of around 1150 was enlarged in 1180 by the addition of a west front and towers and the creation of north and south aisles. Around 1457, St. Mary's was almost doubled in size with the building of a great perpendicular aisled choir.

During the Civil War, nearly 200 years later, St. Mary's was used by the parliamentarians as a forward position for bombarding the castle. Inevitably, the castle batteries returned the fire, destroying the beautiful medieval choir and north transept. The church steeple and bells collapsed in 1659, 14 years after the bombardment. Within 10 years, enough money had been raised both nationally and locally to repair and rebuild the nave, St. Nicholas aisle

and the central tower. The western and central parts of St. Mary's were thus restored to approximately their pre-1450 dimensions, but the north transept and medieval choir have never been rebuilt.

Almost 200 years passed before further major restoration, by Ewan Christian, took place between 1848 and 1850. The numerous wooden galleries and box pews that had for long cluttered the interior were removed and the building regained some if its earlier spaciousness. The four belfry bells were replaced by a peal of eight, augmented in 1979 by two smaller bells from Christ Church in Vernon Road, a former chapel-of-ease to St. Mary's that was demolished in that year. The clock in the central tower, visible from most parts of the Old Town, was installed in 1856.

The latest important restoration of St. Mary's was undertaken in 1950, under the direction of George Pace. Since then, the Friends of St.

St. Mary's Parish Church

Mary's have set themselves the never-ending task of helping to preserve the fabric of this ancient parish church. On 27th September 1993, the Lady Chapel project was begun and this was completed and dedicated by John Habgood, Archbishop of York on 6th February 1994. The ruined sections of the pre-Civil War church are still visible at the eastern end of the main churchyard, silent witnesses to the fearful destruction of 1645. Beyond is the east churchyard, containing the grave of Anne Brontë (see page 5). Since the mid 19th century burials have taken place at the Dean Road Cemetery.

For students of church architecture, St. Mary's contains some odd features in the differing pillars in the nave. Some interesting medieval heads are to be seen at various vantage points in the church. Only four of the many former chantry chapels, dating from the end of the 14th century, remain today. They all lead off the south aisle.

Look out on your way up to the Castle for a weatherbeaten sandstone plaque on the garden wall of The Towers, the large battlemented house that is the last building before the Castle fortifications. This plaque commemorates the

The Hinderwell Monument, formerly sited at the junction between Castle Road and Church Lane, accidently demolished by a vehicle.

Hinderwell Memorial Drinking Fountain of 1860, which formerly stood in the roadway at this point in memory of the great Scarborough historian, Thomas Hinderwell. The drinking fountain fell into disuse and was removed many years ago.

20 Scarborough Castle

Scarborough's 12th century Norman castle has a peaceful role today as a major tourist attraction, in marked contrast to its often warlike and bloodthirsty past.

English Heritage's illustrated booklet, entitled 'Scarborough Castle', is recommended. It is on sale at the Castle entrance.

As you repass The Towers on the way back down Castle Road, turn right by the curious little castellated lodge house on to Mulgrave Place. At the end of this short street are curved flights of steps leading up to Castle-by-the-Sea.

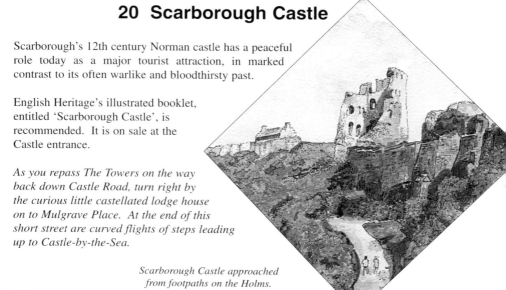

Scarborough Castle approached from footpaths on the Holms.

21 Atkinson Grimshaw at Castle-by-the-Sea

Of the many talented artists attracted to the scenic beauties of the Scarborough coastline, none enjoys such a national and international reputation as John Atkinson Grimshaw, who lived with his wife and family at Castle-by-the-Sea on Mulgrave Place from 1876-79.

Grimshaw's popularity, both in his lifetime and again today, over a century later, was based on the evocative 'moonlight' paintings which he perfected during his Scarborough years. His principal local patron and landlord was a wealthy retired brewer, Thomas Jarvis, who lived in The Towers, facing Castle Road. Castle-by-the-Sea, Grimshaw's seaside bungalow home, is to the rear of his patron's more substantial property.

Perhaps the most significant memento of Atkinson Grimshaw's four year residence at Castle-by-the-Sea is the lofty and spacious central room (the dining room of the present-day guest house) with its top-lit glass roof, clearly designed with an artist's requirements in mind. The massive carved mantelpiece in this room and unique tiled fireplace surround – reputedly hand-painted by the artist himself – were installed during Grimshaw's occupation. He also built the curved double flight of steps leading up to the castellated bungalow, probably incorporating an elaborate stone balustrade in the 1870's, which has since disappeared. Exotic plants were grown by the artist in the conservatory – then running round three sides of the building – some of which provided pigments for his paints.

Four typical examples of Atkinson Grimshaw's Scarborough 'moonlight' paintings are in the permanent collection at the Crescent Art Gallery. Perhaps the most dramatic is 'The Burning of the Spa Saloon', painted soon after Grimshaw's arrival from Leeds in 1876. This magnificent painting is believed to include (in the foreground) portraits of Grimshaw himself, Thomas Jarvis and members of their two families.

From the north end of Mulgrave Place you can admire the view over Scarborough's North Bay and the beautiful coastline towards Ravenscar and Whitby.

Your final destination on this Heritage Walk is the site of the first Methodist chapel in Scarborough at which John Wesley himself preached during the 18th century. Retrace your route along Church Lane, between the main and east church yards of St. Mary's and at the junction with Paradise, turn right and descend the steps behind St. Mary's. This will bring you to Church Stairs Street and just above the first house on the right is approximately where this early chapel once stood.

22 John Wesley and Church Stairs Street

John Wesley, 'the Father of Methodism' was a frequent visitor to Scarborough between 1759 and 1790, making a total of 14 visits. He was particularly fond of the chapel, which local Methodists built as their first permanent meeting place on Church Stairs Street in 1772. Wesley described this building as 'the most elegant square room which we have in England', preaching to 'elegant congregations' there on four occasions between 1772 and 1790. The chapel occupied a site, which is now an extension of St. Mary's graveyard on the right of Church Stairs Street as you descend to Longwestgate, adjoining some post-war council housing.

By the 1830's, local support for Methodism had outgrown the limited facilities on Church Stairs Street and the Blacksmith's Arms, on Queen Street, was purchased for £2,000. In 1840, the first Queen Street Chapel, designed by James Simpson was erected on vacant land adjoining the Blacksmith's Arms, which was itself re-named the Castle Hotel at about this time. (The Castle Hotel has since been demolished after being damaged by fire. The site is now occupied by Blackfriars House, so called because at one time there was a Dominican Priory on this site). The chapel of 1840 was shell-damaged in the 1914 bombardment of Scarborough and then destroyed by fire a few months later. The present-day Queen Street Methodist Central Hall, by G. E. Withers, with its distinctive twin cupolas and somewhat Byzantine appearance, was built after the 1914-18 war on the same site and opened in 1923.

Wesley's own scratched inscription – 'Watch and Pray – Wesley V. D. M.' – on a small pane of glass, believed to have come from the Church Stairs Street Chapel, can be seen in the upper gallery at the Rotunda Museum of local history on Valley Road.

To get back to the town centre, turn right at the bottom of Church Stairs Street and proceed along Longwestgate and Friar's Way for 500 yards to the T-junction with Queen Street. Turn left here passing what was the Talbot Hotel and the Queen Street Methodist Central Hall. At Newborough turn right for town centre destinations.

Old cottages on Church Stairs Street.

Suggestions for Further Reading

Baker, Joseph Brogden (1882). A History of Scarborough. Longmans, Green and Co.

Bayliss A & P (2001). Architects and Civil Engineers of Nineteenth Century Scarborough.

Bentley, Phyllis (1969). The Brontës and their World. Thames and Hudson.

Berryman, Bryan (1972). Scarborough As It Was. Hendon Publishing.

Binns, Jack (1996). "A Place of Great Importance". Scarborough in the Civil War. Carnegie, Preston.

Binns, Jack (2001). The History of Scarborough North Yorkshire. Blackthorn Press.

Crouch D & Preston T (Eds). Medieval Scarborough. (Yorkshire Archaeological Society, Occasional Paper No 1, 2001).

Dore, Simon (1984). Moonlight on Scarborough. (Atkinson Grimshaw). Reprint of article in Country Life (July 5 1984). Available at the Crescent Art Gallery.

Edwards, Mervyn; Editor (1966). Scarborough 966-1966. Scarborough and District Archaeological Society.

Fairlie, Gerrard & Cayley, Elizabeth (1965). The life of a Genius. Hodder & Stoughton.

Fieldhouse, Raymond & Barrett, John (1977, revised edition). The Streets of Scarborough. Scarborough and District Civic Society.

Foord, Sydney, M.M., M.B.E. (1970). Scarborough Records. Typescript copy in Scarborough Reference Library.

Gérin, Winifred (1959). Anne Brontë. Thomas Nelson.

Goodall, J.A.A. (2000). Scarborough Castle. English Heritage.

Hinderwell, Thomas (1798. 1811, 1832). The History and Antiques of Scarborough. The 1978 edition was printed by W. Blanchard, York.

Horspool, Maurice (1982, 3rd edition). The Stones of St. Mary's.

Laughton, Tom (1977). Pavilions by the Sea. The Memoirs of an Hotel Keeper. Chatto & Windus.

Lord, Genevieve W. (1984). Scarborough's Floral Heritage. Scarborough Borough Council.

Marsay, M. (1999). Bombardment.

Pevsner, Sir Nikolaus (1966). The Buildings of England: Yorkshire, the North Riding. Penguin Books.

Pritchard, J. Laurence (1961). Sir George Cayley. Max Parish.

Rowntree, Arthur; Editor (1931). The History of Scarborough. J. M. Dent.

Whittaker, Sir Meredith (1984). The Book of Scarborough Spaw. Barracuda Books.

Many of the above publications are available in the Reference Library on Vernon Road.

The Millennium Stone 2000
in St. Mary's churchyard.